SPYMAKER SPYING CODE BOOK

Sandy Ransford lived in London and worked in publishing before becoming a full-time writer. She has written many books for children, including titles on conservation, puzzles and jokes, games and activities, animals and riding; as well as a number of stories. She now lives in rural mid-Wales with her architect husband, two ponies, two pygmy goats, two sheep and two cats.

Sophie Goodwin graduated with an MA in Illustration and Animation from Kingston University in 2005, and lives and works in London.

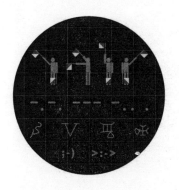

the science of...

SPYMAKER SPYING CODE BOOK

SANDY RANSFORD

Illustrated by Sophie Goodwin

MACMILLAN CHILDREN'S BOOKS

First published 2007 by Macmillan Children's Books
a division of Macmillan Publishers Limited
20 New Wharf Road, London N1 9RR
Basingstoke and Oxford
www.panmacmillan.com

Associated companies throughout the world

ISBN-13: 978-0-330-43981-7

Text copyright © Sandy Ransford 2007
Illustrations copyright © Sophie Goodwin 2007

The right of Sandy Ransford and Sophie Goodwin to be identified as the
author and illustrator of this work has been asserted by them in accordance
with the Copyright, Designs and Patents Act 1988.

1 3 5 7 9 8 6 4 2

A CIP catalogue record for this book is available from
the British Library.

Typeset by Nigel Hazle
Printed and bound in Great Britain by Mackays of Chatham plc, Kent

CONTENTS

1. WHAT IS A CODE? WHAT IS A CIPHER?

Although we often lump them together as ways of hiding secret messages, codes and ciphers are different things. A code substitutes different words, numbers or symbols for letters, words, or sometimes whole sentences. These may be used quite randomly, but the people using them recognize them so they can be used again. A code needs a code book – a kind of dictionary – which lists the words or symbols used, with their meanings. This is the disadvantage of codes, for if code books are found by the wrong people, the codes listed are no longer secret and are therefore useless. For this reason, code books used by the navy are traditionally bound in lead. If they are likely to be captured by the enemy, and the codes discovered, they are thrown overboard, where they quickly sink to the bottom of the sea.

1

A cipher is a system in which each letter of the alphabet is replaced by another letter, number or symbol. The two systems are often confused, and the most famous code of all, Morse, is, in fact, a cipher!

A code is not necessarily secret. Our ordinary writing can be considered a code. It's a means of conveying information between people who understand it. Texting is a kind of code, too. People who aren't in the know often don't understand it!

2

But a cipher is always secret, for its function is to convey information secretly. When two people trying to communicate with each other understand how a cipher works, and which symbols stand for which letters, they can make up any message.

The ancient Romans used gestures as codes, in much the same way as we do today. But whereas we use the 'thumbs up' sign to mean all is well, the Roman emperor who used this sign at the gladiatorial games was signalling that the victor should kill his opponent. We use the 'thumbs down' sign to show that things are not going well, but the emperor used it to tell the victor to spare his opponent's life.

Years ago, when nearly all men wore hats, raising the hat was a polite way of greeting someone. But how many people realized that the habit had developed from the practice of medieval knights of raising the visor

3

on a helmet of a suit of armour, which, of course, the wearer would only do if he were in the presence of a friend?

Some gestures are understood universally. In almost every country in the world, a hand held up with the palm facing forwards means 'halt', and a beckoning hand means 'come here'. Even domestic animals understand gestures. If you wave a clenched fist with the index finger extended at a cat about to jump on your table, or a dog which is getting ideas about pinching your sandwich, they generally realize that you mean 'no'.

Trades and professions also use codes. Have you ever seen a magician who 'reads people's minds', or performs tricks with cards? He or she often has an assistant, who passes on information in code, though we, who are not in on the secret, don't notice. For example, with cards, an ace might mean 'yes', a king, 'no'. Or an object might be chosen in a room, while the 'thought-reader' is absent. When he or she returns, the accomplice points to various things, and the 'thought-reader' identifies the correct one. This can be done by arranging beforehand that, say, the fifth object the assistant points to will be the chosen one.

Price tickets in antiques shops are another good example of the everyday use of codes. If you've ever been in an antiques shop, you may have been puzzled by the labels on the articles for sale. Instead of prices, as you would expect, they often have apparently meaningless letters written on them, such as 'ME'. This is a code used by the dealer to remind him or her of the price paid for the object. It works in the following way. You take a ten-letter word in which no letters are repeated. This might be the antiques dealer's name, let's say it's Palmerston. You write out the word with numbers below, like this:

PALMERSTON
1 2 3 4 5 6 7 8 9 0

So ME would be £45. TN.EN would be £80.50. When a customer is interested in an item, the dealer checks the label to see how much he or she paid for it, so they can then add on an appropriate amount to calculate the selling price.

In the days when travellers and gypsies walked round the countryside, looking for work or asking for charity, they, too, had a code system with which they left messages for the next traveller so they would know what kind of reception they might expect from the people at a particular house. These coded signs are called patrins, and they looked something like this:

▦ = Danger!	λ = This place is no good
○ = Nothing here	⊙ = They call the police here
⋁⋁ = Beware of the Dog	▣ = Householder may use force
○ ○ ○ = Coins - they may give you money	△ = Too many tramps have been here

Sometimes the patrins passed on quite a lot of information, and a traveller who went that way later might use it to tell the people's fortune, and amaze them by how much they knew!

The American Indians used a code based on smoke signals. These could be seen for miles across the plains. The number of puffs of smoke that went up spelt out the message.

In the days before wireless and telegraph, people in Britain used bonfires on hilltops to pass on signals. Sometimes whole chains of bonfires were lit, and this system was re-created for the Queen's Silver and Golden Jubilees. People also signalled to each other by standing on the top of hills and waving their arms. This was the basis for the semaphore system of signalling with flags.

During the Napoleonic Wars, when people near the south coast of England lived in fear of invasion, villagers rang church bells to warn of approaching danger. They were rung to warn of other threats to their safety, too, such as floods. Bells can also ring out other messages. A tolling bell indicates a funeral, and the age and sex of the dead person can be communicated by it: nine strokes for a man, six for a woman, three for a child, followed by the number of years they had lived. Joyous peals of bells are rung to indicate a celebration, such as a wedding. Church bells were rung when the end of fighting in the First and Second World Wars was announced.

Another 'code' which is part of the everyday life of many people is shorthand – the system of symbols that secretaries and reporters use to take down information much more quickly than if they had to write it out. We think of shorthand as being a modern invention, but amazingly a form of shorthand was first used 2,000 years ago by a Roman slave called Tullius Tyro. The early Christians, who were often persecuted for their beliefs, used a version of it to communicate secretly among themselves. 'Modern' shorthand is also fairly ancient – it was invented in 1588 by Dr Timothy Bright.

2. SOME FAMOUS CRYPTOGRAPHERS

A cryptographer is someone who makes a cryptogram, which is a message conveyed by a cipher. Over the centuries there have been some very famous cryptographers.

Roger Bacon
1214–92

Roger Bacon was an English scientist and philosopher, who seems to have been involved in the invention of gunpowder, the magnifying glass, the microscope and the telescope. He also left a manuscript, which was bought by an American, Dr Voynich, in 1912. The manuscript appeared to have been written in medieval Latin or Greek, but when Dr Voynich took it to various

ancient language scholars, none of them was able to read it. Since that time a number of cryptographers have tried to decipher the manuscript, but failed. It seems Roger Bacon managed to construct an unbreakable cipher!

Giovanni Battista della Porta
1538—1615

This Neapolitan invented a cipher based on a block of letters, as shown here:

A	D	G
B •	• E	• H
C •	• F	• I
J	M	P
K •	• N	• Q
L •	• O	• R
S	V	Y
T •	• W	• Z
U •	• X	

When writing the cipher, the letters are replaced by a symbol which depends on the position of that letter in the grid. So

$$A = \lrcorner$$

$$B = \underset{.}{\lrcorner}$$

$$C = \lrcorner_{.}$$

and so on.

Della Porta's cipher has been modified to form a version called the Rosicrucian cipher, which is very easy to use, and looks like this:

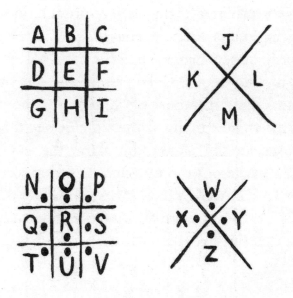

In this cipher, **A** = **⌐J** as before,

but **B** = **U**

and **K** = **>**

Giovanni Battista della Porta also developed more complicated ciphers, one of which was used by Napoleon.

Blaise de Vigenère
1523–96

This Frenchman invented a very ingenious cipher based on an alphabet table, shown right. Each line across starts with the letter of the alphabet following the one that started the previous line.

To encipher a message, you need a key word that has no repeated letters. It can be of any length. The number of letters in the word determines how many of the alphabets in the table are used in the cipher. Let's use the key word SEND. Write out the message. Let's suppose it is: CONTACT ARRIVING HEATHROW FRIDAY. You write the key word above the message as many times as it fits, like this.

S E N D S E N D S E N D S E N D S E N D S E N D S E N D S
C O N T A C T A R R I V I N G H E A T H R O W F R I D A Y

Vigenère Tableau

Letters of message

	A	B	C	D	E	F	G	H	I	J	K	L	M	N	O	P	Q	R	S	T	U	V	W	X	Y	Z
A	A	B	C	D	E	F	G	H	I	J	K	L	M	N	O	P	Q	R	S	T	U	V	W	X	Y	Z
B	B	C	D	E	F	G	H	I	J	K	L	M	N	O	P	Q	R	S	T	U	V	W	X	Y	Z	A
C	C	D	E	F	G	H	I	J	K	L	M	N	O	P	Q	R	S	T	U	V	W	X	Y	Z	A	B
D	D	E	F	G	H	I	J	K	L	M	N	O	P	Q	R	S	T	U	V	W	X	Y	Z	A	B	C
E	E	F	G	H	I	J	K	L	M	N	O	P	Q	R	S	T	U	V	W	X	Y	Z	A	B	C	D
F	F	G	H	I	J	K	L	M	N	O	P	Q	R	S	T	U	V	W	X	Y	Z	A	B	C	D	E
G	G	H	I	J	K	L	M	N	O	P	Q	R	S	T	U	V	W	X	Y	Z	A	B	C	D	E	F
H	H	I	J	K	L	M	N	O	P	Q	R	S	T	U	V	W	X	Y	Z	A	B	C	D	E	F	G
I	I	J	K	L	M	N	O	P	Q	R	S	T	U	V	W	X	Y	Z	A	B	C	D	E	F	G	H
J	J	K	L	M	N	O	P	Q	R	S	T	U	V	W	X	Y	Z	A	B	C	D	E	F	G	H	I
K	K	L	M	N	O	P	Q	R	S	T	U	V	W	X	Y	Z	A	B	C	D	E	F	G	H	I	J
L	L	M	N	O	P	Q	R	S	T	U	V	W	X	Y	Z	A	B	C	D	E	F	G	H	I	J	K
M	M	N	O	P	Q	R	S	T	U	V	W	X	Y	Z	A	B	C	D	E	F	G	H	I	J	K	L
N	N	O	P	Q	R	S	T	U	V	W	X	Y	Z	A	B	C	D	E	F	G	H	I	J	K	L	M
O	O	P	Q	R	S	T	U	V	W	X	Y	Z	A	B	C	D	E	F	G	H	I	J	K	L	M	N
P	P	Q	R	S	T	U	V	W	X	Y	Z	A	B	C	D	E	F	G	H	I	J	K	L	M	N	O
Q	Q	R	S	T	U	V	W	X	Y	Z	A	B	C	D	E	F	G	H	I	J	K	L	M	N	O	P
R	R	S	T	U	V	W	X	Y	Z	A	B	C	D	E	F	G	H	I	J	K	L	M	N	O	P	Q
S	S	T	U	V	W	X	Y	Z	A	B	C	D	E	F	G	H	I	J	K	L	M	N	O	P	Q	R
T	T	U	V	W	X	Y	Z	A	B	C	D	E	F	G	H	I	J	K	L	M	N	O	P	Q	R	S
U	U	V	W	X	Y	Z	A	B	C	D	E	F	G	H	I	J	K	L	M	N	O	P	Q	R	S	T
V	V	W	X	Y	Z	A	B	C	D	E	F	G	H	I	J	K	L	M	N	O	P	Q	R	S	T	U
W	W	X	Y	Z	A	B	C	D	E	F	G	H	I	J	K	L	M	N	O	P	Q	R	S	T	U	V
X	X	Y	Z	A	B	C	D	E	F	G	H	I	J	K	L	M	N	O	P	Q	R	S	T	U	V	W
Y	Y	Z	A	B	C	D	E	F	G	H	I	J	K	L	M	N	O	P	Q	R	S	T	U	V	W	X
Z	Z	A	B	C	D	E	F	G	H	I	J	K	L	M	N	O	P	Q	R	S	T	U	V	W	X	Y

Key alphabet

The first letter of the message is C, and the key word letter above it is S. This means that you use the S alphabet. Go down the key alphabet at the side until you find the letter S. Put a ruler under this line so you don't get confused. Now look along the alphabet that runs along the top until you find the letter C. Move down the C column until you reach the S alphabet. The cipher letter is U.

The second letter of the message is O and the key letter above it is E. Find the E alphabet, put your ruler under it, and find the O on the alphabet that runs along the top. The cipher letter is S. If you continue in this way, the message eventually reads U S A W S G G D J V V Y A R T K W E G K J S J I J M Q D Q. The letters can be all run together, or divided into blocks of four or five to make the cipher even more difficult to crack. Note that with this cipher the same letters of the message are not necessarily represented by the same cipher letters, whereas different letters may be. Sneaky, eh? Despite being over 400 years old, this cipher is so effective that it has remained the basis for many successful ciphers used right up to modern times.

Francis Bacon
1561–1626

Strangely, another man called Bacon was also interested in ciphers. This one was a contemporary of William Shakespeare, and is believed by some people to have written some of his famous plays. Bacon was fascinated by codes and ciphers and invented one based on the typographical errors which were very common in the printed books of his time. At that time, the letters I and J, and U and V, were interchangeable, so each had only one symbol. His cipher was based on the following:

A	aaaaa	I & J	abaaa	R	baaaa
B	aaaab	K	abaab	S	baaab
C	aaaba	L	ababa	T	baaba
D	aaabb	M	ababb	U&V	baabb
E	aabaa	N	abbaa	W	babaa
F	aabab	O	abbab	X	babab
G	aabba	P	abbba	Y	babba
H	aabbb	Q	abbbb	Z	babbb

There are two stages in enciphering a message using Bacon's cipher. First of all you need a written passage. Overleaf is one from Shakespeare's *The Tempest*:

Full fathom five thy father lies;
Of his bones are coral made:
Those are pearls that were his eyes:
Nothing of him that doth fade,
But doth suffer a sea-change
Into something rich and strange.

In the passage, certain letters are marked, either by setting them in bold type, as we've done here, or by sticking a pin through them, or by underlining them. Write out the message in capitals in groups of five letters, retaining the bold letters, and ignoring the punctuation, like this:

FULLF AT**HOM** FIVET HY**FAT** HE**R**LI
ESOF**H** I**SBO**N ESARE CORAL **M**ADET
HOSEA **R**EPEA RLSTH **A**TWE**R** EHISE
YE**SN**O **T**HING OF**H**IM THATD **O**THFA
DEBUT **D**OTHS UFFER **A**SEAC HANGE
INTOS OMETH INGRI CHAND STRAN

Taking each group at a time, and ignoring the actual letters in the group, write a small 'b' for each letter in bold type, and a small 'a' for each letter in ordinary roman type. Thus, for the first three groups, you get: baaab, aabbb, aaaaa, which, if you check the alphabet, gives you

S, H, A. Can you work out the rest of the message? (Answer on page 77)

Samuel Pepys
1633–1703

Pepys wrote a famous diary between 1660 and 1669, which described vividly life in seventeenth-century London (including the plague of 1665, the fire of London in 1666, and fascinating details of life at Court). But not many people realize that the diary, which was not intended for publication, was written in a code which was not deciphered until 1825. Pepys used a kind of shorthand which had been invented by Thomas Shelton in the middle of the seventeenth century.

Leonardo da Vinci
1452–1519

The famous artist and inventor kept detailed notes of his inventions. To keep them secret, and safe from prying people who might want to steal his brilliant ideas, he wrote them in a form of Greek, and also in 'mirror' writing, so they had to be held in front of a mirror before anyone could read them.

Lord Baden-Powell
1857–1941

Best known for founding the Boy Scout movement in 1908, Baden-Powell was a soldier who served in India, Afghanistan, Africa and the Boer War. During the First World War, he worked as a spy. Pretending to be an entomologist (someone who studies insects), he drew tiny, detailed plans of enemy fortifications, which he hid in intricate drawings of butterflies' wings.

3. CODES FROM ANCIENT TIMES

Egyptian hieroglyphs

We now know that the picture writing of the ancient Egyptians was just a different way of conveying information, but no one knew how to make sense of hieroglyphs for many centuries after the fall of their civilization. It wasn't until the early nineteenth century, after the discovery of a carved piece of rock that became known as the Rosetta Stone, that scholars managed to decipher the hieroglyphs. The stone was covered in writing in three different alphabets: the hieroglyphs, a simplified version of them called demotic, and Greek. Eventually, using the Greek, and a bit of trial and error, scholars learned how to read the hieroglyphs. Even at the time the Egyptians used this language, most people could neither read nor write, so the information the hieroglyphs contained was hidden from them, too. Only the scribes, the priests and the ruling class would have been able to read them.

This hieroglyph spells out:

KLIOPATRA

Oghams

The early Celtic tribes of Ireland, Scotland and Wales used a system of secret writing called Oghams. It was based on a straight, horizontal line, with short, straight lines drawn across it. The

original alphabet had only 20 letters, and looked
like this:

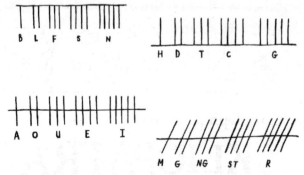

Examples of this kind of writing can still be seen
on early tombstones. People used the Oghams
system for centuries, and Charles I was believed to
have used Oghams for secret communications with
Irish chieftains.

You can use a modified version of Oghams to
send your own messages. Here's an updated
version, with all 26 letters of the alphabet:

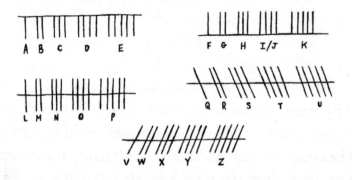

You could adapt this to use sticks and stones from the garden with which to create messages. Here's yet another version of the alphabet which you can 'write' with sticks and stones:

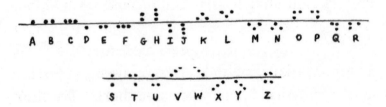

Passports

It was the French who first used passports, during the reign of Louis XIV (1643–1715). They gave them to foreign ambassadors when the ambassadors visited France, and the passports were a bit like letters of introduction, which made travelling around easier for the foreigners. What they didn't realize was that each passport contained a lot of secret information about its owner, which those to whom it was presented could 'read'. For example, the colour of the passport indicated the country that its owner came from: yellow for England, green for Holland, red for Spain, white for Portugal.

The shape of the passport indicated the owner's age. Those under 25 had a round passport. If they were aged between 25 and 30 they had an oval one, and aged between 30 and 45, an octagonal one. There was a ribbon around the top of the passport, the length of which showed whether the owner was single, married or widowed. Punctuation after his name indicated his religion. A full stop meant he was a Catholic, a comma meant he was a Protestant, a dash meant he was Jewish. Markings on the card were used to describe a man's physical appearance: tall, short, fat or thin; his character – whether he was cheerful, friendly or bad-tempered – and whether he was rich or poor. So when the owner presented his passport to a stranger, that person could tell an awful lot about him before he even struck up a conversation.

Heraldry

Heraldry is a bit of a mystery to most of us. It concerns coats of arms, of which the best known is the royal coat of arms, with the lion and the unicorn. But there are many others. The main part of a coat of arms is the shield, which in the language of heraldry is called an *escutcheon*. To those in the know, the different parts of each coat of arms have a meaning, and convey information about the family whose arms it is. Heraldry is also used on flags, such as the royal standard, which flies above buildings when the Queen is in residence. You could make up your own coat of arms based on what you know about your family. For example, if one of your parents is an artist you might incorporate a paintbrush and a palette on one quarter. If your family comes from a town on

the coast, you could have a boat. You could also add something that you are particularly interested in – a book if you like reading, one of your pets if you like animals, even a football if that is your passion!

Signalling by sound

When the Romans built Hadrian's Wall across northern England in AD 126, they put long, hollow pipes inside it in order to communicate between sentry posts, using a method a bit like Morse code. A system of long and short taps conveyed the message. Morse code as we know it (see page 37) wasn't invented until 1837.

Traditional African drummers used a similar code. Their drums were made from hollowed-out logs, which they beat with wooden mallets, using long and short beats, and high and low tones to convey the message. Often the message was beaten out very quickly, and it could be heard up to 20 miles away. Other drummers then relayed it onwards, so information could travel at speed over long distances.

International Code of Signals

Ships at sea have used flags to send messages for centuries. There was a flag for each letter of the alphabet, and one for each of the digits from zero to nine. Because some messages would be very complicated to send and receive by this system, single flags also conveyed certain messages. For example, the flag for O indicated 'man overboard'; the flag for V meant 'I need help'. The flag for P, the Blue Peter, means the ship is about to sail.

Ships also use other signals in emergencies. They may fire guns at one-minute intervals, sound sirens, or send up flares.

Pilots also have a system of signals which can be

spread out on the ground to pass information to those in the air. A triangle means it is safe to land, an L shape means a plane requires fuel, a single line like a figure 1 means someone is injured and needs a doctor.

4. CREATING A CODE

You and your friends can create a number of simple codes very easily. You can then communicate with each other, but the rest of the world won't have any idea of what you're saying!

Clothes

Yes, you can use your clothing to pass on a message! Provided everyone concerned understands the signals, this might be a colour code or one concerned with items of clothing. For example, wearing a red jersey or T-shirt could mean, 'I think they're on to us, look out.' Blue might mean, 'Follow the suspect.' Yellow might mean, 'I need a place to hide for a while.' White might mean, 'All is going well.' You and your friends can decide between you what you want different colours to signify. Try to avoid the obvious, such as red for danger and green for all clear, as sneaky people may easily be able to rumble your code!

But you don't necessarily need to use colours. For example, the following could give signals: wearing a hat, wearing sunglasses, a badge on your lapel, a belt on your trousers or skirt, or the way you tie a scarf round your neck.

Body language

Body language simply means actions like scratching your head, blowing your nose, folding your arms, coughing, rubbing your eyes, sitting with one leg crossed over the other, and so on. Here are some examples you might like to use or adapt:

Scratching your head with your right hand means *Yes*

Scratching your head with your left hand means *No*

Blowing your nose means *Don't tell them who I am*

Pulling at your ear means
Enemies listening, be careful what you say

Coughing means
Danger, take care

Standing or sitting with your right leg crossed over your left means
Follow the person talking now when he/she leaves

Standing or sitting with your left leg crossed over your right means
The person talking is lying

Blinking your eyes rapidly means
Leave immediately

Folding your arms means
This/these is/are the suspect(s)

You can indicate the number of suspects by the number of fingers you leave showing when you have your arms crossed.

Book codes

If you and your friends have identical copies of the same book (a dictionary, a Bible or a school textbook, for example), you can use them to send coded messages. Suppose you wanted to send the following message: SUSPECT JOHN IS ENEMY AGENT, and you were using copies of an English dictionary.

Look up the word 'suspect'. It might appear on page 1164, column 1, entry no. 10. So the code for 'suspect' would be 1164 1 10.

'John' might appear on page 582, column 2, entry no. 19, so its code would be 582 2 19.

If you encode a message in this way, and keep your code book secret, the code is unbreakable. But if the code book falls into the wrong hands, someone would find your code easy to decipher. For this system to work, the books must be the same edition. You can check this with the information on the back of the title page.

Making your own code book

You might like to create a code book of your very own. First of all you need to think of the words you are most likely to be sending in a message, such as 'agent', 'danger', 'suspect', 'meeting', the days of the week, local places such as the park or the cinema, times of day, and so on. Then you

31

need to think of a code language to use. Let's say it's things to eat and drink. So your code book might contain terms like this:

agent	milk
danger	tea
suspect	bread
meeting	cake
Monday	apple
Tuesday	pear
Wednesday	banana
Thursday	orange
Friday	grape
Saturday	lemon
Sunday	strawberry
in the park	sandwich
at the cinema	pie

So the message AGENT MEETING SUSPECT SUNDAY IN THE PARK would become MILK CAKE BREAD STRAWBERRY SANDWICH, and unless they had access to your code book, no one would have the faintest idea what it meant!

Using a code grille

A code grille allows you and your friends to send secret messages hidden in innocent-looking letters.

Each of you needs a copy of the same grille, and then you simply write a letter putting the keywords where the gaps in the grille are.

Here's an example. It looks perfectly ordinary, but when you put the grille (see next page) over it, the message is revealed.

Dear Amy,

How are you? It seems a long time since we met. I hope you haven't caught a cold or flu this winter.

Dad is complaining of molehills on the lawn, yet does nothing about them. But Mum and I like the creatures. On the subject of animals, did you see John and his dog on TV tracking rabbits? More news on this when we meet.

Come and see us soon.

Love,
Brenda

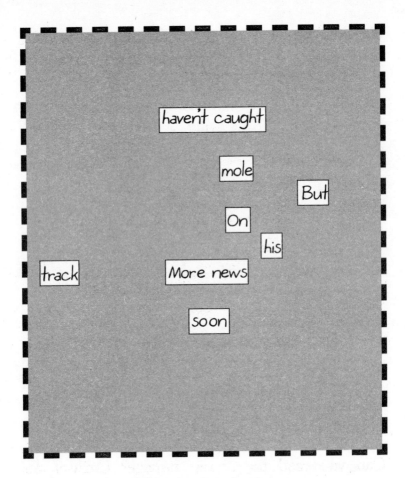

Using pin holes

You can also hide a message in an ordinary letter by sticking a pin through the letter just above or below the word you want. This is a quick and easy way of sending a secret message, but it isn't very safe. If someone found the letter, it wouldn't take them long to discover the holes, and, once they did, they're very likely to spot that they indicated a message.

Dear James,

How's your new job coming along? I hope the boss is treating you well.

I'll come over at the weekend, my bike wants its brakes fixing, so I might have to catch a bus. I'll see how it goes.

Did you see the new Star Wars film? I hear it's very good.

See you soon,

Love,

John

Can you read the secret message? (Answer on page 77)

Using invisible ink

Though this isn't really a code, it is a useful way of sending a secret message. You write a message in invisible ink, and then write an ordinary letter on the same sheet of paper, using different lines for

35

the message and the letter. When your contact receives the letter, all they have to do is to warm it by holding it near a radiator or a light bulb, and the hidden message will appear.

Lots of different things can be used for invisible ink. The following all work well: a sugar solution (dissolve a teaspoonful of sugar in a glass of water), lemonade, apple juice, orange juice, lemon juice, grapefruit juice, vinegar, salt (dissolve a teaspoonful in a glass of water), bicarbonate of soda (dissolve a teaspoonful in a glass of water).

Work out what you want to say before you write your message. The wooden end of a matchstick, or the clip on the top of a plastic ballpoint pen, works well as a pen. You simply dip your pen in the 'ink' and write. The only problem is that you can't see what you're writing, which is why you need to work it out carefully beforehand!

5. CLASSIC CIPHERS

The most famous cipher of all must be Morse, which, confusingly, is called a code, even though it is actually a cipher! It was invented by an American called Samuel Morse, as an alphabet which could be used with his telegraph system for sending messages, and was first used in 1844. As most people know, Morse code replaces each letter of the alphabet, and the digits from 0 to 9, with a system of dots and dashes.

The great thing about this system is the number of ways in which it can be used. It can be written down, as it is overleaf, or in a number of other ways: tapped out; sent as a series of flashes of light using a lamp or torch, or even a mirror reflecting sunlight; or sent as a series of blasts on a whistle. Originally signallers sent telegraphic messages in Morse code by using a buzzer.

A	.-	M	--	Y	-.--
B	-...	N	-.	Z	--..
C	-.-.	O	---	1	.----
D	-..	P	.--.	2	..---
E	.	Q	--.-	3	...--
F	..-.	R	.-.	4	....-
G	--.	S	...	5	.....
H	....	T	-	6	-....
I	..	U	..-	7	--...
J	.---	V	...-	8	---..
K	-.-	W	.--	9	----.
L	.-..	X	-..-	0	-----

As well as being written as dots and dashes, Morse can also be turned into small and large symbols of various kinds, such as these:

The classic distress signal, SOS, in Morse code is: three dots, three dashes, three dots, which is very easy to remember and to transmit.

Semaphore

Semaphore uses different arm positions to indicate letters. To make it easier to see, the signallers usually hold flags. The colour and design of the flags aren't important.

Scytales

Scytales were devices used by the ancient Romans, Greeks and Egyptians for sending secret messages. They consisted of a long, continuous strip of parchment or papyrus which was wound round a wooden stick like a bandage. The message was carefully written on the parchment so each letter appeared on one of the turns. Then the strip of parchment was removed from the stick and rolled up into a spool, which the messenger hid. The receiver of the message needed an identical stick on which to wind the strip when he received it, and he could then read the message.

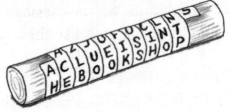

You could send a message to a friend in this way today, using a narrow strip of paper wound round a pencil.

Crossword cipher

This needs a crossword-type grid with black and white squares. The person sending the message and the person receiving it must have identical copies of the grid. Suppose the message is:

TRUCKS CARRYING ROCKETS CROSSING BORDER AT MIDNIGHT ON THURSDAY. HIDE AT CHECKPOINT TO NOTE NUMBERS.

You write out the message straight across, starting at the top left corner and working downwards, running the words together without gaps or punctuation. If your message is a letter or two short of the number of white squares, add a couple of extra letters, known in code and cipher language as 'nulls'.

To send the message, you read the grid downwards in columns. So the message shown in the grid would be written out like this:

CRO DCT TA SDDOA TU R OSE NYH M
URC RNT EOB RKI I HCN ENA HIK YTG G
DPO CIS THU OTE K CBM REI R SN OITSA
ES GRR TNN

The person who received it would write it into their copy of the grid and would then be able to read it easily. But it would be impossible without the grid.

Transposition and substitution ciphers

A very simple transposition cipher is to write your message backwards. For example

ERTAEHT ERIPME EHT NI 61F TAES REDNU SI EGAKCAP EHT

Can you read it? It wouldn't fool a cipher expert for long! But suppose you saw this list of words? Try reading down the initial letters, and then reading up the last letters, and see what you get.

SAUSAGES
MOTHS
INDIGO
THUMB
HARE
IRISH
SALT

(Answer on page 77)

Railfence cipher

The railfence cipher is another transposition cipher. It is a bit more complicated, but really very simple to work out. Suppose your message is:

MEET COURIER PADDINGTON
WEDNESDAY NINE PM

Write it on two lines in an up-and-down zigzag, starting on the upper line, like this:

M E C U I R A D N T N E N S A N N P
E T O R E P D I G O W D E D Y I E M

Now write out the message again in the two lines as it appears:

MECUIRADNTNENSANNP
ETOREPDIGOWDEDYIEM

You wouldn't recognize it, would you? To make it less cumbersome, divide the letters into blocks of five:

MECUI   RADNT   NENSA   NNPET
OREPD   IGOWD   EDYIEM

As there's one letter left over at the end, it's added on to the last 'word'. To decipher such a message, simply divide it into two long 'words' and write them in the up-and-down zigzag again. The cipher is called railfence because it goes up and down, like the kind of fencing that used to be seen at railway stations.

The box or route cipher

You can use any size grid for this, but people often use a five-by-five square. Write the message in the box in any order you like. Here we've written it across from left to right, working down the box.

$$S \quad E \quad N \quad D \quad M$$
$$E \quad T \quad H \quad E \quad C$$
$$O \quad D \quad E \quad B \quad O$$
$$O \quad K \quad Q \quad U \quad I$$
$$C \quad K \quad L \quad Y \quad A$$

Because the message is one letter short of the squares in the box, a false letter, or 'null', has been added. Any letter will do as a null.

When you write out the cipher, you could read down the columns, from left to right:

SEOOC ETDKK NHEQL DEBUY MCOIA

or from right to left:

MCOIA DEBUY NHEQL ETDKK SEOOC

either of which is very confusing if you don't know what the cipher is! You can read up one column and down the other, in a zigzag up or down the grid, or even in a spiral, so the letters would read

SENDM COIAY LKCOO ETHEB UQKDE

But there's a danger here, as the spiral begins by spelling out the first word, so it might be better to do it backwards, starting MDNES.

Column cipher

This is another simple but effective way of hiding a message. Suppose the message is ARRANGE MEETING WITH M ON TUESDAY. You could write it in two columns, like this, going down the first column and back up the other:

A	Y
R	A
R	D
A	S
N	E
G	U
E	T
M	N
E	O
E	M
T	H
I	T
N	I
G	W

Or you could write both columns downwards. If you now read these columns across, you can write the letters in blocks of five, like this:

AYRAR DASNE GUETM NEOEM
THITN IGWAB

The last two letters are nulls. Again, the message is very well hidden, and could only be discovered by someone who knew the system, or by a very determined and clever cryptanalyst!

Substitution ciphers

These are probably the simplest to work out. They are the kinds of ciphers that substitute a figure, another letter, or a symbol for each letter of the alphabet. So A might be 1, or Z, or some kind of symbol. Provided you know which cipher is being used, you can decipher messages created in this way quite quickly. Morse and semaphore are substitution ciphers.

Julius Caesar used a cipher in which a letter three places on in the alphabet is substituted for the 'real' letter. So A is represented by D, B by E, and so on. A variation of this, which is often called a Julius Caesar cipher, uses a key word in which all the letters are different. Suppose you use the key word KITCHEN. You write this over the first seven letters of the alphabet, and then write out the remainder of the alphabet, omitting the letters in KITCHEN.

KITCHENABDFGJLMOPQRSUVWXYZ
ABCDEFGHIJKLMNOPQRSTUVWXYZ

The last six letters of the alphabet are the same in both the 'real' and the cipher alphabet, but as they are not used very often (see page 62), this doesn't really matter.

Graph cipher

A French woman spy in the First World War used a graph cipher to send messages to Switzerland embroidered on cloth. It must have taken hours of painstaking work. The result zigzags up and down like a graph, but if you draw lines across from the upper and lower points, and print the alphabet down the left-hand side, the points of the graph can be seen to represent letters. This was discovered by counter-espionage agents, who later arrested the French spy.

Here's an example of a graph cipher, first without the alphabet in place, and then with it. Can you read what it says? (Answer on page 77)

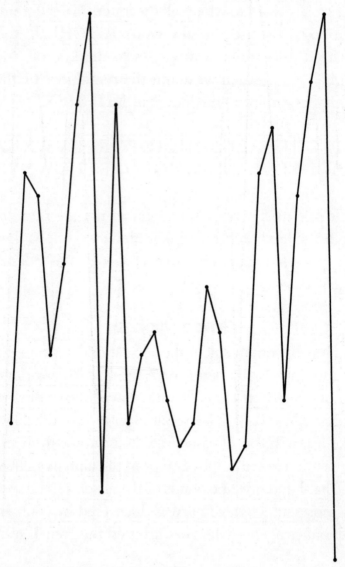

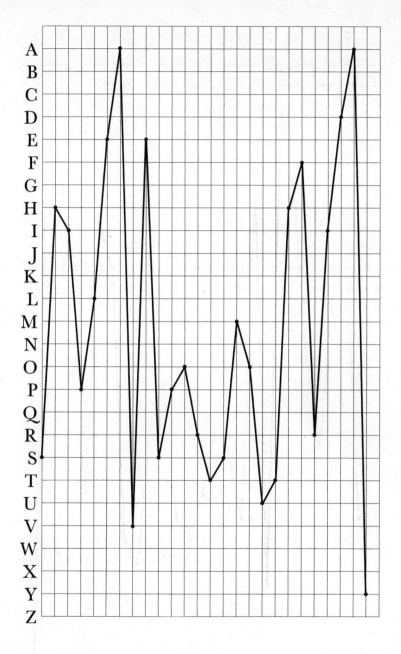

6. CREATING A CIPHER

You can use any of the ciphers you've read about in this book to send your own messages, or you could change them slightly to create a unique cipher of your own. If you're new to ciphers, and don't want to try anything complicated, why not start by using a simple substitution cipher where A = 1, B = 2, and so on.

If you used this cipher, what would this message be? (Puzzle answers on page 78)

3 1 14   25 15 21   11 5 5 16   1
19 5 3 18 5 20

Or you can send an innocent-sounding (but perhaps a bit odd!) letter in which the first (or last, or second, or whatever you decide) letter of each word spells out the message you wish to send. What do you think the sender of this note is trying to say?

Tall Henry Ibbotson never knew that Harry Edwards yelled silly untruths so proclaiming every clever trick Yankees only used.

It seems very strange, but it's really very simple!

Or what about this, based on a real letter received by Sir John Trevanion, who was imprisoned in Colchester Castle during the English Civil War? The letter was innocent enough, but Sir John knew that the third letter after each punctuation mark spelled out a message, which contained instructions to help him escape. You can use this method to send a message of your own.

Try deciphering this one.

Dear Sally,
Tim, when he called, emerged from the car with a walking stick. He told me he had sprained his ankle playing football, but it was getting better.
   You must come over soon, the orphan lamb, Leslie, fed with a bottle, is absolutely lovely. Day by day he gets bigger, Anne says he follows her like a dog. Two of us take turns to feed him, poor thing gets confused!

Ben sends his love. What did he give you for your birthday? Betty got a great book.

Pat says she is coming home soon. When she does, what do you want to do? Best to have a plan, I think, though she may not like it!

Hoping to see you soon
Alice

If you've learnt Morse code (see page 37), you could use it in a different way. For example, A is •— but you could show it as a small upside-down V followed by a larger one, like this:

∧ Λ

You could also show it as little drawings, such as a small face and a large one, a small cat and a large one, and so on. You can have no end of fun creating your own cipher! What do you think this says?

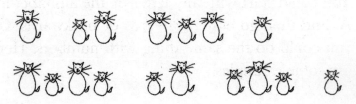

Another simple way of disguising your message is to write it out backwards, and then divide the letters into blocks of five. What do you think this says?

YLLUF ERACM IHHCT AWYPS ASINW ORBNA MRIEH TNGKL

Because this message doesn't divide equally into five, four false letters or 'nulls' have been added at the end.

Or you could try one of the grid ciphers. Draw a five-by-five square box, and write out your message in it, going across from left to right and top to bottom. Fill in any extra squares with nulls. Then write out the message in blocks of five letters reading down the columns from left to right. Try this:

TEAOR HMNMA EYTBI EPOAN NLBTN

What about creating your own substitution cipher? You could start with any letter of the alphabet for A, and then go either forwards or backwards. Or you could do the same thing with numbers. Here are some examples.

1	2	3	4
A = H	A = P	A = 35	A = 84
B = I	B = O	B = 36	B = 83
C = J	C = N	C = 37	C = 82
D = K	D = M	D = 38	D = 81
E = L	E = L	E = 39	E = 80
F = M	F = K	F = 40	F = 79
G = N	G = J	G = 41	G = 78
H = O	H = I	H = 42	H = 77
I = P	I = H	I = 43	I = 76
J = Q	J = G	J = 44	J = 75
K = R	K = F	K = 45	K = 74
L = S	L = E	L = 46	L = 73
M = T	M = D	M = 47	M = 72
N = U	N = C	N = 48	N = 71
O = V	O = B	O = 49	O = 70
P = W	P = A	P = 50	P = 69
Q = X	Q = Z	Q = 51	Q = 68
R = Y	R = Y	R = 52	R = 67
S = Z	S = X	S = 53	S = 66
T = A	T = W	T = 54	T = 65
U = B	U = V	U = 55	U = 64
V = C	V = U	V = 56	V = 63
W = D	W = T	W = 57	W = 62
X = E	X = S	X = 58	X = 61
Y = F	Y = R	Y = 59	Y = 60
Z = G	Z = Q	Z = 60	Z = 59

Using these examples, can you read the following messages?

1. DOLU JHU FVB IYPUN AOL RLF

2. G IPX ELKW TL CLLM P CLT PJLCW

3.   37 49 48 54 35 37 54   42 51
         43 47 47 39 38 43 35 54 39 46 59

4.   73 80 84 63 80   69 84 82 74 84 78 80
     64 71 81 80 67   66 65 70 71 80   83 60
                 78 84 65 80

If you're feeling ambitious, you can create acipher using a key word (see pages 12 and 47). Choose a word in which every letter is different, for example NORWICH. Write this word over the first seven letters of the alphabet, and then write the letters not contained in the key word in alphabetical order over the rest of the alphabet.

NORWI CH A BDE FG J K LMPQS TUVXYZ
A B CDE FGH I J K LMNO P QR S TUVWXYZ

The last letters of the alphabet again remain the same, but because they are not used very frequently, this doesn't matter. What does this message say?

SIFF GNPY B ANUI
SAI HKKWQ

With this kind of cipher, no one will be able to work it out if they don't know the key word.

Text messages

Texting is a kind of code in itself, and you probably have your own form of text 'shorthand' that you use to contact your friends. But to make it more secret, use a substitution cipher. If you use one where the letters are replaced by numbers, you can replace any numbers in the message with letters. For example, if you wanted to send this message:

Waiting for news, please text.

You might send it like this:

W8ing 4 nws pls txt.

But most people would be able to understand it quite easily.

So use a simple substitution cipher, A = 1, B = 2, etc., and it comes out like this:

23 H 9 14 7   D   14 23 19   16 12 19
20 24 20

The average person texting would find it much harder to decipher! You can devise your own cipher to use with your text messages so that only the people you want to understand it will be able to do so.

Cipher wheel

This is another way of creating a cipher. You can make a cipher wheel with some thin card and a split-pin fastener (the kind you push through and then open out to hold the card in place). You need a large disc and a smaller one. On the large disc divide the edge into 26 sections, and letter it round clockwise from A to Z. If you want to use numbers in your cipher, add the numbers from 1 to 26 under the letters.

Divide the smaller disc into 26 sections and letter it round anti-clockwise. Mark the letter A section with an arrow. Make a hole in the centre of both discs, place the smaller on top of the larger, and fasten them together with the paper fastener.

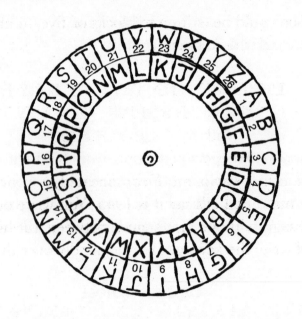

There are two ways you can use the wheel. One is to choose a key letter to go with your message. Let's say it is G. Turn the A of the inner disc so it points to the G on the larger one. Then, using the letters of the smaller disc as the 'real' ones, and those of the outer disc as the codes, you can read off your code letters very simply.

So the message *Meeting is on Friday the fourth* would come out like this:

U C C N Y T A   Y O   S T   B P Y D G I
N Z C   B S M P N Z

which could be written in blocks of five, to make it more difficult to crack:

UCCNY TAYOS TBPYD
GINZC BSMPN ZKMNT
(with four nulls at the end)

The other way is more complicated, and needs a key number. Let's say it is 1945. You write out the message without any spaces between the words, and write the key number repeatedly over the top, like this:

1 9 4 5 1 9 4 5 1 9 4 5 1 9 4 5 1 9 4 5 1 9 4 5 1 9

M E E T I N G I S O N F R I D A Y T H E F O U R T H

To encipher the message, turn the smaller disc until the arrowed A is opposite the first figure of the key number, that is, 1. Look for the first letter of the message on the inner disc, that is, M. Opposite it, on the larger disc is the letter O, which becomes the first letter of the enciphered message.

Then turn the inner disc so the arrowed A is opposite the next digit of the key number, that is, 9. The next letter of the message is E, which is opposite E on the outer disc. So the encoded message begins O E.

Then turn the inner disc so the A is opposite the next digit of the key number, 4.

The next letter of the message is also E; this time the letter opposite it on the larger disc is Z. Because you use a key number, the same letters in the real message are not encoded by the same cipher letter, which makes the cipher more difficult to crack. The enciphered message now begins O E Z.

You continue like this until you have encoded the whole message. Can you work out what it will be? It's a complicated but very safe cipher you can use in your most top-secret missions!

Pin-men cipher

Have you read any of the Sherlock Holmes stories? In one of them, 'The Dancing Men', in a book called *The Return of Sherlock Holmes*, Holmes solves an intriguing cipher based on little pin-men figures. You could create one of your own, like this:

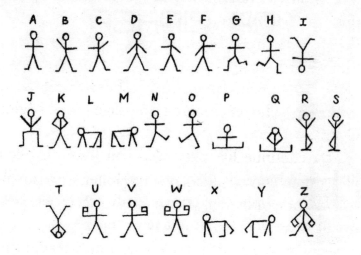

In this cipher, what does the following message say?

61

7. CRACKING A CODE OR CIPHER

When you create a code or cipher, or write in code or cipher, you make the decisions, you are in charge of it. But when you try to crack someone else's, it's not so easy. You may recognize the code or cipher used, but you will have to do a bit of detective work if you don't.

First of all, look at the letters, numbers or symbols. Are any of them repeated often? The one that is repeated the most often is likely to be E, because E is the letter that appears most often in English. (It may be different in other languages.) The letter that appears next often is T, and the next are A and O. Here are the letters of the alphabet in the order of the frequency in which they appear.

E, T, A, O, N, R, I, S, H, D, L, F, C, M, U, G, Y, P, W, B, V, K, X, J, Q, Z.

People have also worked out how often certain words are used. Here is a list of some of the most common words in the frequency with which they are used: the, of, and, to, a, in, that, is, I, it, for, as, with, was, his, he, be, not, by, but, have, you, which, are, on, or, her, had, at, from.

Obviously, if a symbol, letter or number stands on its own, it must be either A or I. A three-letter word which appears a lot is likely to be 'the' or 'and'; a two-letter word may well be 'of', 'to', 'in' or 'is'.

So first you have to check how often letters, or combinations of letters, appear.

Some combinations of letters are more common than others. Apart from the words listed above, the most commonly used combinations of two letters are as follows: th, in, er, re, an, he, ar, en, ti, te, at, on, ha, ou, it, es, st, or, nt, hi, ea, ve, co, de, ra, ro.

If you are dealing with a simple substitution cipher, this is how you would start to decipher it. Here's an example, from a sentence in *The Secret Agent's Handbook*.

17 3 9   17 11   23 29 31 47 29   41 17 11
27 11 39 39 3 15 11   7 31 29 7 11 3 25 11 9
19 29   41 17 11   25 11 41 41 11 37   17 11
47 31 43 25 9   29 31 41   17 3 45 11

5 11 11 29   39 31   39 43 37 33 37 19 39 11 9

Take a look at it and note down how many times each number appears.

17   appears six times.

 3   appears four times.

 9   appears four times.
    (and always at the ends of words).

11   appears 14 times.

23   appears once.

29   appears six times.

31   appears five times.

47   appears twice.

41   appears five times.

27   appears once.

39   appears five times.

15   appears once.

 7   appears twice.

25   appears three times.

19   appears twice.

37   appears three times.

43   appears twice.

45   appears once.

 5   appears once.

33   appears once.

The number that appears most often (14 times) is 11, so that number is likely to stand for E. Write E in the message wherever 11 appears.

17 3 9   17 E   23 29 31 47 29   41 17 E
27 E 39 39 3 15 E   7 31 29 7 E 3 25 E 9
19 29   41 17 E   25 E 41 41 E 37   17 E
47 31 43 25 9   29 31 41   17 3 45 E   5 E E 29
39 31   39 43 37 33 37 19 39 E 9

Now, leaving the next most frequently used numbers for the time being, look at the 9, which always appears at the ends of words, and twice after the E. This means it could well be a D. So try putting D in where the 9s are.

17 3 D   17 E   23 29 31 47 29   41 17 E
27 E 39 39 3 15 E   7 31 29 7 E 3 25 E D
19 29   41 17 E   25 E 41 41 E 37   17 E
47 31 43 25 D   29 31 41   17 3 45 E
5 E E 29   39 31   39 43 37 33 37 19 39 E D

So the first word cannot be 'the', but the fourth word could be. So let's assume that 41 is T, and 17 is H, and put in both those letters.

H 3 D   H E   23 29 31 47 29   T H E
27 E 39 39 3 15 E   7 31 29 7 E 3 25 E D   19 29
T H E   25 E T T E 37   H E   47 31 43 25 D
29 31 T   H 3 45 E   5 E E 29   39 31
39 43 37 33 37 19 39 E D

It's beginning to look like a message now, isn't it?
Look again at the first word. What do you suppose
the vowel in the centre is? It could be A, I or O to
make a word, but 'had' would make sense, whereas
the others wouldn't, so let's try assuming that 3 is
A and put all the As in.

H A D   H E   23 29 31 47 29   T H E
27 E 39 39 A 15 E   7 31 29 7 E A 25 E D
19 29   T H E   25 E T T E 37   H E
47 31 43 25 D   29 31 T   H A 45 E   5 E E 29
39 31   39 43 37 33 37 19 39 E D

Let's now look at the second and third most
frequently used numbers, 17 and 29. We've
discovered that 17 is H, but what about 29?
According to the table, the next most frequently
appearing letters in English are T, A, O and N.
We've used T and A, which have fitted in and
made sense, so what about O and N? Look again
at the message. The number 29 appears at the end

of three words, which means that in English it's unlikely to be O. So let's try putting N in.

HAD HE 23 N 31 47 N THE
27 E 39 39 A 15 E 7 31 N 7 E A 25 E D
19 N THE 25 E T T E 37 HE
47 31 43 25 D N 31 T H A 45 E 5 E E N
39 31 39 43 37 33 37 19 39 E D

Look at the two short words in the third line, '19 N', and fourth line, 'N 31 T'. The first word could be 'in' or 'on', but the second is unlikely to be 'nit', so let's assume that 19 is I and 31 is O.

HAD HE 23 N O 47 N THE
27 E 39 39 A 15 E 7 O N 7 E A 25 E D
IN THE 25 E T T E 37 HE
47 O 43 25 D N O T H A 45 E
5 E E N 39 O 39 43 37 33 37 I 39 E D

The penultimate (next to last) word could be 'so' or 'to', but we've already found T, so let's assume 39 is S.

HAD HE 23 N O 47 N THE
27 E S S A 15 E 7 O N 7 E A 25 E D IN
THE 25 E T T E 37 HE 47 O 43 25 D

N O T   H A 45 E   5 E E N   S O
S 43 37 33 37 I S E D

Now look at the ninth word. This could be 'better', 'getter' or 'letter'. 'Letter' is the most likely. So let's try L for 25, and R for 37.

H A D   H E   23 N O 47 N   T H E
27 E S S A 15 E   7 O N 7 E A L E D   I N
T H E   L E T T E R   H E   47 O 43 L D
N O T   H A 45 E   5 E E N   S O
S 43 R 33 R I S E D

Have you noticed anything else about the cipher? A was 3. Several of the letters that appear less frequently are much higher numbers, such as 43, 45 and 47. So you might have cracked your cipher, as, if it follows a simple progression, the higher numbers would stand for the last letters of the alphabet such as U, V, W, X, Y and Z. Look at the third word. If you're right, 47 might be one of the last letters of the alphabet. It begins the last word on the third line also. Let's try W, which would (what was that? The last word on the third line could be 'would') give us this:

H A D   H E   23 N O W N   T H E

27 E S S A 15 E   7 O N 7 E A L E D   I N
T H E   L E T T E R   H E   W O 43 L D
N O T   H A 45 E   5 E E N   S O
S 43 R 33 R I S E D

So let's try U for 43.

H A D   H E   23 N O W N   T H E
27 E S S A 15 E   7 O N 7 E A L E D   I N
T H E   L E T T E R   H E   W O U L D
N O T   H A 45 E   5 E E N   S O
S U R 33 R I S E D

And while we're looking at these higher numbers, what about V for 45 in the fourth word from the end, making 'have'? So if U is 43, V is 45, W is 47 and A is 3, it looks as if the cipher begins with 3 and then proceeds in twos. And all the numbers are odd ones. Try working it out like this, and see if you can solve the remaining letters in the cipher. (Answer on page 78.)

To crack a cipher, you need to know about the frequency of letters and words, but you also need to spend a bit of time trying out various guesses. You may need quite a lot of patience too!

8. CODE AND CIPHER PUZZLES

See how many of these codes and ciphers you can crack. (Answers on page 79.)

1. This cipher looks like a long shopping list, but the prices are a bit odd! And why do some of the items have two prices? (This is a clue!)

Bread 5p
Ice cream 1p
Apples 1p
Jam 3p
Carrots 5p
Macaroni 7p
Pudding 3/4p
Cornflakes 10p
Turnips 5p
Wine 3p

Watercress 9/10p
Beans 3p
Fish 1p
Meat 2p
Lentils 5p
Pastries 4p
Walnuts 1p
Milk 2p
Lettuce 1p
Salmon 3p
Aubergine 3p
Pears 2p
Tomatoes 2/6p
Fruit pie 6p
Honey 4p
Vinegar 3p
Waffles 3/4p
Cheddar 7p
Broccoli 8p
Cat food 7p
Garlic 2p
Yogurt 1p
Coriander 6p
Pumpkin 6p
Eggs 2/3p
Cherries 2p
Sprouts 6p

2. The clue to this one is text messages.

2 2 9 23 21

3. And here's another. Remember the substitution cipher that uses a key word? Think about that. The clue to the key word is: one of the two most famous English universities.

BRSTQNY YNUQ MNBR
ANNH LNW

4. This one is a column cipher. What does it say?

NSEAX TTUMR EDEAT YIFNI
GRMSI TDJDU ANYEA

5. Don't let this one give you the hump! (See page 38 for a reminder.)

6.   To solve this one you have to think in reverse!

LIRPA   DRIHT   NOMTH   GINDI
MHTUO   MYLPG   NIVIR
RAENI   RAMBUS

7.   And what about this weird list of words? You
could go up and down it.

WIN
ALTO
TWO
CRESS
HACK
STOIC
ULTRA
SUCCUMB
PAINT
EVER
CLEO
TRIP
SHARE
CLEVER
LONELY
OWL
SPACE

8. Can you solve this one?

S Y I C E E T E O N T I G A
P C R L C N R D N O T N H M

Try aligning the second string of letters under the first slightly differently and looking up and down them .

9. Do you remember the body-language code on pages 29 and 30? If you were following it, and you saw someone sitting like this:

what would they be trying to tell you?

10. You will need your cipher wheel to solve this one. The key letter is P.

M H X J V H X L   R B V Y X L E K
O L K B Y L   X I P M B T H C J

11. And here's another cipher-wheel conundrum using the second kind of cipher. The key number is 7863.

ITLL ZTLKC ZN BMBZYD
WBCLD FJ SUDY

12. This one might look totally mind-boggling.

TTOSM RHNTE AGMNE
IIIET NNDGA

But write it out like this:

T T O S M
R H N T E
A G M N E
I I I E T
N N D G A

Try reading it up or down, from either end, and see what you find.

ANSWERS TO PUZZLES

Chapter 2 Some Famous Cryptographers
Francis Bacon

'Shakespeare was a great writer.' (There are four 'nulls' at the end.) (page 17)

Chapter 4 Creating a Code
Using pin holes

'The boss wants to see you very soon.' (page 35)

Chapter 5 Classic Ciphers
Transposition and substitution ciphers

'Smith is the boss.' (page 42)

Graph cipher

'Ship leaves Portsmouth Friday.' (page 48)

Chapter 6 Creating a Cipher

'Can you keep a secret?' (page 50)

'Think they suspect you.' (The message is spelt out by the first letter of each word.) (page 51)

'Meet Tuesday noon at tea shop.' (page 51)

'Take care.' (page 52)

'Their man Brown is a spy – watch him carefully.' (page 53)

'The enemy plan to bomb a train.' (page 53)

'When can you bring the key?' (page 55, 1)

'J. has left, we need a new agent.' (page 55, 2)

'Contact HQ immediately.' (page 55, 3)

'Leave package under stone by gate.' (page 55, 4)

'Tell Mary I have the goods.' (page 56)

Cipher wheel

OEZLSVX WI UQ ZJAAEC PWA VUJNHB. (page 60)

Pin-men cipher

'I need help.' (page 61)

Chapter 7 Cracking a Code or Cipher

'Had he known the message concealed in the letter he would not have been so surprised.' (page 69)

Chapter 8 Code and Cipher Puzzles

1. 'Diamonds in safe. It will be open Friday night.'
2. 'Big Brother is watching you.'
3. 'Destroy your code book now.'
4. 'Next meeting midday Saturday first June.' (There is one 'null' at the end.)
5. 'Gold leaving Hatton Garden in white van marked Higgins Plumbers.'
6. 'Submarine arriving Plymouth midnight Mon third April.'
7. 'Watch suspects closely, report back soon.'
8. 'Spy circle centred on Nottingham.'
9. 'Follow the person talking now when he/she leaves.'
10. 'Disguise yourself before shadowing their agent.'
11. 'Your house is bugged, leave at once.'
12. 'Meet agents on midnight train.'

SPYMAKER
SPYING
ACTIVITY
BOOK

GABY MORGAN

YOU CAN BE A SPY!

Develop your sky skills by solving puzzles,
unravelling clues and breaking codes in this
SPY-TASTIC activity book.

Remember: this must not fall into enemy hands!

SPYMAKER
SPYING
HANDBOOK

SANDY RANSFORD

FOR YOUR EYES ONLY!

Do you have what it takes to be a top spy?
Could you spot an enemy agent and trail them?
Could you disguise yourself so they won't recognize you?

As a secret agent, you will often encounter
tricky situations. After reading this book you will
have tactics for dealing with them at your fingertips.
Escaping from a locked room, using secret codes and
writing invisible messages are just a few of the skills
you will master. But remember: a top agent never
reveals their sources . . .

HOW TO BE AN
ASTRONAUT

AMANDA LI

Everything you ever needed to know about space and how to become an astronaut

A fast, fact-filled romp through the history of space travel, from early astronomers gazing at the stars, via the history of flight and the breaking of the sound barrier, to Armstrong and Aldrin walking on the moon in 1969.

Packed with colour pictures and lots of photos from the Science Museum's incredible collection, featuring early images of space, pictures of the Earth taken from space and fantastic equipment used on the space shuttle.

A must for anyone whose ambition is to reach for the stars!

THE INFINITY CODE

E. L. YOUNG

**Will Knight, 14: Inventive genius.
Creates cutting-edge gadgets (S.T.O.R.M.-sceptic)**

**Andrew Minkel, 14: Software millionaire
(and fashion disaster). Founder of S.T.O.R.M.**

**Gaia Carella, 14: Brilliant chemist with a habit of
blowing stuff up (usually schools).**

**Caspian Baraban, 14: Gifted astrophysicist.
Obsessed with the immense forces of space
(equally immense ego).**

Will mocks S.T.O.R.M.'s plan to combat global problems, but then they uncover a plot to create a revolutionary weapon. Will swallows his doubts as they race to Russia to confront the scientific psychopath with a deadly power at his fingertips.

The first book in the S.T.O.R.M. series, *The Infinity Code* is a gadget-packed high-adrenalin adventure.

L. BRITTNEY

Nathan is an actor in the same company as Will Shakespeare. A skilled acrobat with many other talents, he catches the eye of England's Spymaster General. Recruited as an agent – and partnered with fearless spy John Pearce – Nathan is trained at a School of Defence in the arts that will keep him alive.

His first mission takes Nathan Fox to Venice – into the eye of an explosive situation involving the formidable General Othello . . .

The first title in the Nathan Fox series

A selected list of titles available from Macmillan Children's Books

The prices shown below are correct at the time of going to press. However, Macmillan Publishers reserves the right to show new retail prices on covers, which may differ from those previously advertised.

All Pan Macmillan titles can be ordered from our website, www.panmacmillan.com, or from your local bookshop and are also available by post from:

Bookpost, PO Box 29, Douglas, Isle of Man IM99 1BQ
Credit cards accepted. For details:
Telephone: 01624 677237
Fax: 01624 670923
Email: bookshop@enterprise.net
www.bookpost.co.uk

Free postage and packing in the United Kingdom